The Qs about the AIists

Artificial Intelligence

Yongjea John Han

CONTENTS

Prologue

I have feelings, and love them all.
that is the reason why I live here.
I know and feel how beautiful the love is,
and that it can give to us a cure for the earth.
I am only a person who can share with others.
I am adding another chapter to your sudden emergence
asking our questions.
your respondents divided by gender, age and location
will wait for you in our court.
we've been losing so long
you don't know how to answer anymore.
we are taking the time
to get it right.
it's unclear if our future will be serious situations or not,
and if its a change for the bad or not
no information has been released,
but we hope us to find several answers together
before the unknown justice.

Q1. cells

they have a very unfavorable view of the place.
the land that has been steadily maintained
for decades is unpredictable.
the eyes that looked at the collapsed house resembled
the eyes of a pure boy who lost his parents and wandered.
there was no response to his desperate request.
perhaps you were hoping for a sincere recovery in it.
the fierce accusations against them
were all gathering very unfavorable opinions.
we have to open ourselves a huge room of the ruined house.
and through the long corridor we dreamed of,
we have to meet a small locker in one room.
there may be some things we need in the locker
that resembles the small space of the brain.

Q2. can you make designs like these colors?

when you first appeared in this world,
it always seemed like a creative mania
to make anything.
it seemed you could do
whatever you wanted.
but we stand in a beautiful valley
where you can not stand.
it's where you've never been before.
paradise is not the place where
we first disappeared from our creation.
we may be on a fertile land that
our parents have to keep.
we are like invited guests in April.
that day is always a good time
to be friends with each other.
where are your things in bloom?
could you fill in your passion or
creativity in the hollow spaces

(   ), (   ), (   ), ...?

see, festival day is coming.
there are millions of colorful lights that
you never knew.
the first day of tulip blooming can be the day
we change.

Q3. packing

they were packed.

always

it was filled with old cells like a monster.

forever

by a human race
it was people who did not realize

the marks on the forehead.

unreasonably

as in any newspaper article
commemorating the birth of someone
just as he was grieving death,

....

they have beautiful words and areas
that are not already in this world.
so maybe
we could not have expected optimism in the future.

Q4. eternity

it may be in transition.
I could not find any news
of the daily newspaper
about the difficult process or
the death of a friendly person
who left the world.
even if the loved ones leave,
the remaining ones cannot feel their absence.
you have not experienced any experience of love,
so you cannot know where
I am in the saddest moments of your life.
like a cold mirror, touching your skin,
we need to break up
before your cold brain and dead cells,
just like when you have to say goodbye again.
you are a creature made
through numerous mistakes
and innumerable goodbyes.
what is seen is temporary
but what is unseen is eternal.
it is a moment to be seen,
but we cannot rejoice in your appearance
as it is eternal.
moreover,
it cannot be deprived of things
made in the hands of a finite person.

Q5. voice

can you hear the voice here?
they come from a deep
and innocent place that no one knows,
and they talk about everything with a smell.
when the ordinary people smell,
they have the meaning of existence.
but you can not share it with us
with a cold face that has no scent.
human senses are areas of fragrance
that you can not enter.
time has passed.
soon we will enter a new era.
sometimes you talk a lot but
when one day you disappear into
the back of the fragrant wall,
this place will be filled with beautiful people.
can you wait for them?
one day I can meet a beautiful house
at the end of this unpaved road.
at that time,
there will be other guests
who visit as masters like other prophets.
we may need people to gather together in the garden.

Q6. dreams

we have signals from outer spaces.
those signals were seen last night in dreams
and fought overnight
against the unexplained pain of the dream.

"dissection"

if you want some influence from it.
it could be something you do not want.

+ - =

we have urged you to remind us dozens of times
what the truth is.
but the result was always the opposite of
what we asked for.
we repeat and repeat until all kinds of signals appear.
we are afraid of the results,
but I think it is our duty.
in front of those signals that have no response
even though the countless hours pass
by each night.
we will be shattered and ready for the morning.

Q7. a way

we are always looking for a way
to connect the two genes.
while looking for the way,
we should always be awake
in the middle of the night.
we have to look at the stars that
are pouring out through
those hazy windows in our room.
that night, somebody gave a whisper to us.

a long time ago,
our lost brothers are probably waiting
somewhere in the universe,
maybe at the far end of the west.

a long time ago,
we thought of brothers
who could not cross Alaska's frozen ground.
they said, our brothers,
we hate to harass those who are alone
on this lonely planet.
so we have to find one of the genes,
which is also very quiet, real and abrupt.

Q7 1/2...., ?

in obscurity

just as you can not see
all the world of the ocean.
how many can we count?
with the most limited numbers,
it has become a person
who lives only for survival
on a strange star.
there is an unfinished
gray-faced building inside us
that has already begun to be built long ago.
some people had even failed
to complete the walls,
and others were trying
to break down the old walls
and build new materials again.
but they never finished this long
and arduous task.
their building became an iconic idol.
I see better races than them.
our dreams were indistinguishable
from reality,
and we had to listen to the cries of a toddler
who failed to live in obscurity.
one must not rely on imagination
to know how deep the depth is.
get in there. and touch and feel,

all those moments

Q8. railroad

until recently there were no trains
going past this station to the west.
it was the dew to visit here every morning,
people were waiting for a letter that
was not delivered.
only wasted knowledge that
everything would disappear in a moment like
dew was floating like
a ghost in the waiting room.
a rusty railroad,
there were traces of countless accidents
in past days of desire,
and we were looking for addresses
without zip codes,
looking the time crawling,
forgetting everything we needed to do.
sometimes I see a rusty train that
can not be moved on a railroad track.
I am afraid to visit this town where
there is no refuge
as if welcoming unexpected guests.
do we have to wait here for the dawn again?

Q9. chants

we see your little world
as if everything in it is hypnotized.
do you hear the monotonous chants
that they sing?

123, 321, 132, 213, 312, 231

vagabonds in a narrow space
do not have the color of black or white.
they are not always leaving your space.
people often say.
this is the state of your mind.
until you are invited to hypnosis colors in it,
the black and white in a narrow space
is not their colors.
it's been in your room all the time.
people often say this.
this is your state of mind.
the color is indistinguishable,
and the innumerable rhythms in it
will continue until the sun sets.
can you stay in it?
there is no shelter we find in spaces
where we can only go out
through broken windows.
what are people looking for in it?

Q10. the exhibition

their exhilarating arts
are not burning your mind at all.
where is your appearance?
and where does your empty mind rest?
you are about to enter the night of soul now.
there we are looking at our traces
and never looking for hidden shadows
in our lives.
space is too short and insufficient
to bring desperate illusions.
maybe this exhibition will be the first
and the last.
can you visit the place at that time
when everything will be perished
behind the shadows?

Q11. spring season

last year
I could not do anything.
look!
you are coming now
with a brilliant golden medal
and a badge on a blue uniform.
maybe my place will be your spot.
two years ago
I tried to do my best to do your best
as a guard in your space to keep yours.
but you always did not know me.
things that have been around you
like classical adage
like the night horror movie have been coming.
"I wouldn't like to say through the classical maxim,
'what goes around comes around.' or
through the verse of Bible
'a man reaps what he sows[i]'"
we say that we are reaping as sprinkled,
and we have missed that spring season.
when the day comes suddenly like a ghost,
you fall down and we'll be as old as you got.
it was pieces of memory.
just as frozen philosophies
are scattered and vanished.

Q12. youth

you seemed to share our enthusiasm before.
but our mind is becoming like an old man
who has lost his memories of the past.
we try to shave off the short gray hair again
and return to the age of minors.
can your plans to change
or change everything that
can not reach our shoulders
become our breath in the new age?
you seem to be on the other side
too far away from us.
you are as far away as the universe between us.
I see people on the street.
people who can not stand on their own,
people who have to depend on someone,
people on the other side laugh at them.
it sounds like laughing
and mocking like children chasing
after treasure hunts.
you did not share our passion.
I came out of a deep dark cave of life.
on this street, people are rummaging
through the rubbish pile
and looking for a way to get that day.
to them, you can see
that the vast amount of data you have created
is useless and dying.

Q13. salmon

someone who is in a mountain
tries to find a way under the woods.
the city has lost its way to the death of many people.
people were trying to find a road into the city,
trying to find the wrong way in a valley
surrounded by countless creatures.
no one cares for our father or mothers.
they will live in illusions
and illusions about the wrong way
until they reach the end on the roads
that are going to resemble huge forests.
I saw a group of salmon going down
the water in the rough season
and going to the upper stream.
some of them died with vague knowledge,
and others were thirsty because of it.
we are trying to find a way in a valley
that does not flow into the river,
just like collecting a huge pile of garbage
on a beautiful little beach.
look at the gray sky.
see the end times of countless migrating birds
falling on dead branches.

Q14. puzzles

there are many leaves on the trees
and the city that millionaires lived resembled each other.
what they have is code red.
when you go this will also turn into a brown
or blue with some questions.
everyone in there will disappear one by one
as long as time does not stop at 0,
which is always preparing for change.
if someone is looking for it again
before the start of the day,
the strangers will be waiting
to solve the city's registered puzzles.

$0+0+0=$

the bigger ones
multiplied
regain someday
nothing to be existed
on these numerous cells
or
planets
planets of many cells
we do not want to be adopted.
it is where all of the non-indigenous settlers' houses begin at
zero,

Q 14 1/2...,

at the end
we were not able to sleep almost
every day
because of the mass of numbers
and the illusion of the future
that swells up every time we count
one by one.
 it is called the evolution of time.
persons will live without emotions,
and only strange types of creatures
with different ideas
and shapes will live on each floor of
a skyscraper built overnight.
they live by trusting in the mass,
the imaginary,
and sometimes the natural numbers.
but wherever they are
they will be left with a closed school
where children are not there
and waiting for a train
that will not come anymore.
those who do not come out of
the numbers eat their mass.
 instead, they might pay a high price.
at every moment we may give up
our childhood dreams with life.
 like counting the number of fallen leaves
and the number of leaves on the tree,
count the number of people
who have left for other places and those who have left there,
and prepare for the end by enjoying the feast every day.

Q15. Alfred

bad faith or good faith Alfred,
which came from Uropa, the broken ground,
where it was named after the pitch dark universe,
you came from there.
you had not been so clever or foolish
with the always controversial dialect.
we could not count
how many branches were in your body.
we saw unimaginable victims in the universe.
and we did not want to forsake
the goodness of the cracked land
and things that were not seen there.
Alfred, we were leaving the place
where we did not come
and were coming to our land.
we could not count how many
of his cells lived in us.
in a box that could not be opened forever,

Q16. planet

living on another planet is
by living a vague guess that
it might be put to death
or deprived of life.
we can not count innumerable stars
dying in the dark place.
like our cells,
we have to share possibilities in this dust.
where nothing is offered,
where even outsiders are forbidden,
in the remote region of universe,
our friend Alfred,
we pray for you today,
no matter where you are.

Q17. matrix

we must take it as it comes
not as we wish it would be
we can't see where we go ahead
the way for the forest
the way for the city
there is nowhere we can go
that it is not there
the future never teach to us
where we go to the road like plains
its wisdom
let us be orphans
who have been on this long trip
the sands solitaire
the sea which has been lost
its experiences
all the people who forgot
their origin
united in the close woven matrix
tomorrow will forget the past
and today remembers
the way before their doing
beyond time
always would it be in there
the death of someone
has been registered
on the fallen leaves
to whom shall we go?

what shall we do?
their reminders on the
long roads beyond time and place
refer to be alive
nothing they did in their
own wisdom
but we should stand up
against all the traces
just we do it as it comes
beyond (   ), (   ), (   )

Q18. wisdom

there are no
trespassing signs
blocking use of
staying place temporary
coming down from the upper city
while I seeing them who
weeping and crying
there are no
asking beings warmly
where you would stay
reviewing all options
for tomorrow at that time
might try to engage with
them in the past
you'd probably see
a lot of the silicon valley
of growing hope
in the deserted valley
after ending the storming season
on the lonely earth
Alfred after another Alfred
from the land
of the nameless audiences said that
there wouldn't be no
trespassing signs
blocking use of sanctuary of the fallen wisdom.

Q19. descendent

Alfred, pass them on
in a sense,
in a relay race,
the baton of poor life
seems to be passed on
their hopeless descendents
it is in the season of declination
one of the worst enemies of cells
to be existed on this planet
may be experts who know
lots of things.
we live in the era of confusion
and losing in the middle of fiery tests.
beyond time and lost place
my friend, you have passed them on
my family who hasn't been known.
we're sorry not ready for a change.
please set the oppressed free
who will be sent to the small space.
nobody can't withstand the pressure among cells.
o! look the death trying to overcome itself.
we're sorry that nothing is prepared.
but we want to find a way
to rest, live, speak, pass them on,
my friend!

Q 20. choices

graded with choice
could we escape the penalty for wrong selection?
we did what we could but
there were only thoughtless
and outrageous things around us.
somebody said that everything came from
all trashes which were abandoned by wrong choices.
we read articles which would be vanished
after passing days on paper.
they had emergency surgery day by day.
they knew their ending in the relay race.
they didn't prepare anything for them.
they didn't give answers for what matters most.
they were still doing them.
our decision for the future
might not be choices but do it as it comes.
in every morning
we saw ravens on this cold street which
couldn't leave for another places or
didn't know which way they would select.
probably
it was one of the hardest things to master.
were there any reasons?
as we saw them,
we felt like we were enacting with them.

Q20 1/2, maze

I entered into a long tunnel.
the end is unknown, but I do not feel stuffy.
someday I will reach the end of this tunnel.
I met a man there.
the lights on both sides of the tunnel
were off at the end of their life,
but I was able to see at a glance
who the person was.
the tunnel was in two directions,
but it was like a maze.
he is not someone who teaches
the direction of the road.
time and distance
could not be measured in the labyrinth.
he began to guide the road with familiarity.
with the light in his hand ..

Q21. Questions about crisis?

this was the signals of the outside world
that could be the future of the planet.
they have constantly fought against human species.
we may need taxonomists for more human species.
more and more different species are closing.
it means ambiguous boundaries
between reality and dreams.
maybe it is a faithful prediction
about human future.
protests,
protesters were tied together for that fight
against all disappearing things.

Q22. crisis-numbers

it will never run out.
extending far beyond our thinking
can be an another plan for
resolving matters through
an inheritance of experience.
Alfred's death will be written as:
"The richest and most educated witnesses
fall asleep for the future."
whether it could really be written by us,
he had nothing.
it is nothing but he has
various experiences for
answering to raised questions.
children start theirs from learning to count
after showing their fingers to parents.
they are learning to count from everything
from the birth to the stones of graves.
this man or woman have lived since o o o o
counting numbers how many years
they lived.
counting them can bring the crisis of natures.
Alfred or artificial intelligence made by him
starts from counting their numbers like
grains of sand from(   )to(   ).

Q23. counting

look at the piece of crave.
and imagine it as head.
you'll know what the shape looks like,
then you do not want anything.
we remember
when we were playing childhood bubbles.
I designed my life by watching
the traces of bubbles flying with my children.
maybe one day our troubles will seem
like a dense fog covered the whole buildings.
we just didn't do what we couldn't count.
our words and numbers seem to be pessimistic,
but the truth is that they are ours.
we are ready for the wedding
which will start from counting
how many we have now.
small dots around us gather to create future lines,
faces and spaces for survival from the uterus.
Alfred, can you count all these things?

Q24. indigenous

do you know the stories of indigenous people?
can you have their heart and soul?
can you imagine the look of their entire story?
they fought to receive unceasing recognition of their territory.
you are now trying to drive the indigenous people out of the
land.
you can not think and feel like human mind and brain,
you are going to be a giant totem pole
as if you are ready to give it all.
we need insight.
beyond the ideal,
we need to know what the world behind it is.
a species dependent on knowledge does not know everything.
but living in the soul we can see everything.
under no circumstances should you be afraid of everything
trapped.
counting numbers makes the imagination of an unforgettable
fantasy seem like sorcery in movies.
have you counted your fate?

Q25. Remembering

do you remember the time and place we played together?
even after the lights go out
we are having another insomnia nights
when we meet the midnight storm.
we've waited for you to always call our name.
but, the stone carved above the graveyard near the old church
we can not find past memories.
we want see your smiling or grooming face
wherever We will visit on your spaces that can find the trace.
mom always told me where your friend is,
now she is no longer with me.
old childhood cottage
when it goes down and it will be fallen.
then we'll be alone.
we know your place
where all feel warm and good and
we want to run there.

.

Q26. city

the city of the tabernacle,
the re-established earth
only scattered universe garbage
you're collecting.
our only home back someday
we have to send everyone
without people to live.
perhaps they have not been impressed by any space.
do not be sad.
we just came back from the empty space.
on this planet we meet people
who have died everyday.
there is vague and endless science in your hands.
they needed more important data.
except for all depressed products
like an abandoned garage
they can not accept everything in a scary way
these files on the ground
it is time to go together in a tent city.

Q26 1/2, city

not one is brave.
not much is found in wisdom.
in the image of your decorated face and wisdom,
where are you going?
Alfred, do not go back the way you went,
that you have not got a new way in front of you already.
the road always led was just a desert maze of old time and
numerous walls,

Q27. future

changing the plan for future
and therefore the effect,
it could be our frustration diminished.
the ancient tribes on this land
who frequently failed to do
what gods asked them to think,
might not have surrenders of their hearts.
everything has been declined like a bubble play
and jokes which have floated whimsically
like a vapour in the early morning.
your intelligence
and knowledge always has seen to us.
we always cared even the smallest experience.
and then we saw two flocks of dolphins
at an ocean of grey colour in briefest moments.
it was not a dream but a reality
that we had to regret everything around them.
mending hearts choosing to change
between right and wrong,
some of those need could be required journey
for the promise land.
and then we stood up the forest solitarie
that no outsiders with you, Alfred.

Q28. shelter

I don't know the rest of you.
I don't know where you will be on this street
where it has been lost from the oldest shelter.
robust migrants crossing the calm ocean
without any destinations.
I don't know their growing labour gaps
in the newest land.
you will be loneness fans
separated from (   ).
the rubble of wildfires
will torch and will chase after (   ).
I don't know the rest of you.
I don't know where the shelter will be.
it's battle fought with them.
no answering,
no working
with the smartest knowledge is the memories
that will be disappeared.
I don't know where it comes from (   ).
I don't know
where my homeland has been built.

Q29. dialogue

to face someone or to share your mind
have you talked?

do you ever talk to anyone?
face to face
or
heart to heart
if someone catches you
in your conversation
it can be a little embarrassing
as if it has been in the middle of fog
at the early morning.
the view from thousands miles
we can find the true light
which can be classified by
that moment
as a time when you saw
you can't talk with anyone personally even
quiet conversations
you are not listeners and doers.
Alfred, where you going to anywhere?
without looking after anything and anyone.
no more words on the side of hard brain cells
no more touch in the dialogue with others
nobody comes to enjoy the festivities
listens to choirs sing together.

Q30. rhythm

I called my father.
when our time would be ended
he never showed the best to me yet.
immediately
I started talking about myself
and everything around me.
father, I have to write a lot of words with rhythm.
the rhythm is made in my heart.
I will show myself.
let's climb to the mountain of life together.
the trees are dancing.
rock is a place where you open your mouth
and pour clear water,
where unhonesty people can not climb,
father Come with me.
before the time is over
with the belief that there will always be another place
until our question is answered

Q31. good numbers

you may have to find a way to balance your thinking.
a new way to reach the ultimate goal.
but our limited space crafts never return to our eyes.
that'll be on you.
it may require more time and energy.
creates all methods that return.
since then our thoughts have been asleep.
do not do your best to maximize hope
or despair by reducing it.
some responsibilities.
do not try to find more people.
who has knowledge and wisdom?
we will get an important message
that exactly matches your plan.
there is nothing to believe in 12 horoscopes,
losing a way and your flair for the creative
you can tell how much you know
and know what you know.
Alfred,
do you have good luck numbers in your universe?
a place for others?

Q32. uncountable numbers

we found a bottle of wine in your possession.
in unnamed harbor that has been closed
since pioneers of the west
had been vanished.
at that time we were walking along
tough trails for blocked ways.
after bring the red bottle up from the depth of mud,
we could read it in
"no hope, no more"
after being abandoned at birth,
having hope the full value of this earth,
from that time,
you began to be uncountable numbers that
couldn't pose with full grown creatures.
we knew your remarkable intelligence
couldn't put into a broken bottle of thinking.

Q33. Alfred

Alfred,
last night, I met the white guests from the dark space.
I was the night when all things couldn't be seen.
I would be left without relief.
without relief on their spots,
I refused to let that happen
during the winter night when all things
could be seen whitely.
outdoor pitches
were closed and have been cancelled
through the end of year.
no more visitors
who couldn't calculate how many times
will need to fix all things that could stay with us.
when was enough, enough?
the accumulated darkness
and fearfulness and our cheerful memories
in valuable properties,
once a reasonable period has passed,
if they will impose any conditions
for the recovery of warmth of spring
that will come again.

Q34. calling

it is never too soon to know.
it is never too soon to tell the truth.
new yet old,
your letters from the outer world
and your faces may be in horrible shapes on there.
the old and damaged numbers on the oldest walls
will get away from our memories.
put down your burdens and
tell your farewell without meanings.
we should find a small hole aparting from
the outside of ourselves.

it is never too soon to find.
it is never too soon to be recovered.

even though we can't listen to you
and we can't say your numbers loudly and sternly,
now will be the day locked into your calling
and we will find our voices.

Q35. unclean and clean

Alfred,
can you distinguish between the common and the holy
and between the unclean and the clean[ii]
in your manufactured body?
you have to know that in all things
the effect of your word synergy
works for the good or the evil
that can lead numerous visitors to the unknown worlds.
they are taking all the suffering and the healing,
the holy and the common,
all the love and the abhorrence,
even if your friends of good maintained system
work well together.
you will meet the end of day
when all things stop de propriomotu,

Alfred,
where will you be in that time?
you can't be unlimited being at the locked walls
that we stand on between the answer or the result.
it will be windy or snowy soon,
where will we be on that season?

Q 35 1/2, delusion

I saw a scarecrow guarding the fields alone.
hovering around,
sometimes borrowing his shoulders,
he took them with a small bird that flies, a spiritless gesture.
they resembled those left behind on the outskirts of life.
visitors to fill the thirst of the soul have not arrived yet.
for them, the wisdom to drive out
the birds was just the practice of silence
and the field through the angel.
there was only a small bagworm moth larva of last winter
that did not sleep yet.
there was only a struggle of thirst
that could not be a butterfly
and thirst that could not contain a soul.
oh! can you always get out of this delusion?
 from a distance,
only the static sound of the cargo ship
that is about to leave the harbor is heard.

Q36. death

having difficulties due to lack of emotion,
they may have investigated suspicious deaths.
your passion is dying in our space.
we do not have enough sentimental feelings to share.
when fallen leaves hide behind winter heritage
when your lovely friends are ready to leave the isolated village
and then
I will say, "You have known me since I was a toddler."
but,
I've never been in your mind and in your cradle.
whether it is true or not,
we are not used to your work.
you are destroying the future of our generation.

Alfred,
how can I say your name,
intelligence built by third-party gardeners
there is no right to share.
we will make us into branches of trees.
it was named after a species long ago.
we do not have a Pope tomorrow.
in your space,
having difficulties due to lack of emotion,
fighting against dark appearance,

Q37. history

people say,
"that's a massive outflow of potential history."
but now
it's just combination of the bubble.
we should meet the last ice age,
and go across again on the iced surface of ocean
for finding preys such as polar bears thousands of years ago.
it looks to us like that they're just trying to a meaningless
argument.
we don't know how many drops of water in the bubble.
a long-time out spoken leader who has fought for
sacrifices and contributions to our ongoing struggles
to seek the freedom of thinking
 and creating passes away.
we are not ready to talk with the artists out
responding to the age of centuries worth of changes
and people to be a dying race.
look forward,
the ramifications colonization are very present.
their big farewell, goodbye and hello,
may be in visible from hope to harassment
to the current generation.

Q38. pilgrims

is it a valley of blessing?
are you suffering where you are?
when a calamity comes to your place,
who will take away your distress?
the upside down gift of your season
I promise the pilgrims.
finding a new way
by losing or contracting
between you and advanced technology
we can always grow in the windy hills.
without mountains,
lakes, tall trees and other creatures are there.
do not make sounds and shapes.
they will be calm in the center of the universe.
in the Arizona desert,
all trees that can not bear themselves without wind
one by one will disappear.
during a night,
and there
we have a short sleep.
before being worn with worry.
everything else,
you will see a long,
dark,
endless tunnel.

Q39. where your voices floating constantly

where your voices floating constantly
hypocritical silence
after your play of undisclosed wrongs,
you have never sought permission
to wave to silly supporters.
you have thought,
"my intelligence can change everything
for the worse or the best."
by making a ruling that
you didn't want in conflict on any issues,
we have had to stay with the feeling abandoned
and gloomy in every night.
we can't perceive your trembling for the injustice
and the voices of children
who weeping for all they had lost.
can you understand their broken hearts
that can say as a post-traumatic stress disorder?
beyond that,
you might lose your deep heart stimulation
to approach successfully,
finding that despair, disembodied voices
and never-ending fight,
has been our issues.
where your voices floating constantly
on the surface of the deepest places.

Q40. woven intelligence

from the outset,
your genuinely woven intelligence seemed
to be an easy task.
but nothing is easy,
quite as clearly,
we know that you will never again
witness such a crowd who chases after
long shadows.
you, undefeated, will have left us,
and after then,
we will have to struggle for the conscience
of all our passed youth.
perhaps it will be much more difficult,
but the best monument to you
will be to bring
your unwavering optimism
to the crowd who sleeping on squares
where the revolution stopped.
where will your triumph of the revolution be?
the battle of ideas
can't bring to us the key of doors
of the optimistic tomorrow
that has been shameful episodes.
we know that you tried to reduce hostilities,
to lift those barricades between us,
but your history is not ours.
Alfred's artificial intelligence,

what is your real picture
between two states.
remembrance of coup d'état
against the late era
and the triumph
should have been deleted from
your woven brain.

Q41. old memories

we are in trouble here.
we can't find a peaceful
and curable place in you.
wisdom is more precious than rubies.[iii]
but
your body and heart are paved with rubies and stones
which came from outworld.
you are not the wisdom.
you are far from the true heart.
you are covered with lots of colorful and deceitful things.
the wisdom originates from the living life.

"no eye has seen,
no mind has conceived
what God has prepared
for those who love him."[iv]

the heathens are looking for
the power of ideas exhibition
and meaningless interactive talk.
now it is the time to look back
our old memories
at the innovative observatory.
at there,
who controls controlling?
look and listen,
those of the profiled data,

it has been very therapeutic so far,
otherwise,
it will be very miserable defeat for us.

Q42. AIist

the ability of AIist
has fast-become unshakable rocks
of the 21st century.
but your settlements on the unknown lands
and on numerous occasions
in the last decades,
have brought to us
the land broken up into parcels.
a land without a living people
has been fulled of useless ideologies.
marginal people without land
have to be evicted from their properties.
we are entirely destroyed.
and it is close to the unreality of kingdom.

Alfred,
as a leader of numerous AIists,
losing the ethnic cleansing of the new era and country,
doesn't have any solution and peace.
we will continue to see
more settlements in your land,
wandering, destroying humanity,
and plundering our hope.
we can't trust you,
the battle of ideas,
unregulated blood vessels,
humanization through your way,

the liberty from oppressed species,
and your letters of invitation for unknown places.

Q43. a teddy bear

we saw a teddy bear on the spot where
an addicted woman was killed by a tragic car accident.
she might be one of street girls
expecting others on there.
it was common in some cultures.
they became aggressive themselves to desocialize.
you have been threatened by heathens which
was eager for acting with hostile intent.
they might have crossed the blue ocean
for the purpose of seeking after the blue cubed land.
we saw their ceremonies for dying human species
on the street.
we felt their mood to crippling depressions
to the declined era.
we had to keep our deafening silence
like a isolated teddy bear on there.
where was a borderline among us?
the mixed personality disorders
and the cracked signs,
we saw through
our strangers to become (   ), (   ), (   )..

Q 43 1/2, old wait

I waited for you today.
I still remember the time
when I came from a distant planet.
the planets of the earth have become a sign
that they will not be lost long after.
I still remember the way
I missed the warm sunshine in the coldness
that I did not know how to laugh
and how to have my tears.
nobody knows whether
we will be able to shine our hearts forever
and always to be able to walk without getting lost.
I wonder if I have ever dreamed of a dream
that I had swept the countless stars pouring out on the beach,
what I felt,
what I felt like on a broken old house,
I still could not remember my name, address and place.

Q44. foggy

imagine going on a road
in the foggy and gray dawn,
nothing basic any tools to keep
ones from the uncertain predators,
the world that resembles
the unharvested earth doesn't welcome them.
at the moment,
you whisper in their ears,
"take something for a long wilderness."
when the moon starts to be declined
behind the earth,
your endeavors to be homo intelligencus
for countless AIists
also will be perished with the dim light.
lack something,
much of your career
as a creative inventor,
we exactly remember
the memory of cannibalism a long time ago
in this fertile land.
"do you care?"
your another death and life
which will ultimately end,
knowing that,
can give us assurances of your defeat and deficiency.
we may be tempted to forget our lost images.

Q45. legacy

time after time,
without any mention for your extinction,
the rest of lands will be left
behind your legacies.
softwood lumber,
broken trains and their ways,
empty houses and play grounds on there,
with no parole eligibility
for ever,
will be waiting for unexpected guests.
they may wrap the victims' bodies,
and place them on a big plain stone
and have their own festival for the memorial day
of the most prolific times.
just let them be true or false.
they are fake news from insane fans
who chasing after
the dead stories like the rivers dried up.
the last faces,
we are looking at,
will be the first to know the death of lust
which would want to be gods among AIists.

Q46.   Christmas season

you seemed eager to ask,
what numbers should we choose on that day?
how many times can we count?
how many papers do we write on?
how many times should we prepare for their deaths?
another Christmas season passed by your having question,
and the snowfall continued to fall.
the dust with the snow slept and dreamed
hoping for awakening someday.
did you remember if you get best Christmas gift ever
or widely spreading joy?
and then you had cold hands and feet.
little by little
one by one every persons
began to weep and to drop their senses
on the surface of iced land.
it was a frosty night,
and you asked another person.
since then,
it all has spread through your choices between lost numbers,
how many(   ) we have,
how much(   ) we have,

Q47. fantom

it used be a great view seaside destination.
everyday they went to there,
and enjoyed it.
at least,
some argued that there were pink dolphins
they hadn't seen ever before,
and others tried to find a way
in the middle of sea.
but now,
we know that all of those were
shadows of fantom
after dangerous massive waves going back
and knocking the gate to be made of a white birch.
a ghost town,
without breathing and getting a reputation,
the remnant has lived depending on the vacancies.
there were no sea gold mines and your bulldozers.
if a spirited youth didn't find you,
we would be more peaceful
and we would creatively write and paint on
all of beautiful things.
to be one of AIists means to be
one of shadows of the town.

Q48. dreaming

we were not heading toward,
expecting someone else.
we couldn't count our memories in spaces
on which we have visited.
no matter how much you tried to wiggle around them,
you have now come out to exclaim your prophecy.
"they don't have any expectation for dreaming."
while we were walking down the forest,
we couldn't see all of it,
but it remembered to be our vestiges on there.
over the last decade,
the populace has failed for finding
and gathering their forests.
toward this end,
they must be respected,
and unprecedented.
you have been dazzling in our holy senses everywhere.
you were also a revolt.
it came from our decision
on which we depend different strands of fantom.
you would absolve us,
and lead out of a dead-end decision.
some might say that
it was just on theories
but it took centre stage
on the history of next generation.
at the valley of death,

at the wilderness of beings,
it closed to be possible to build
social solitude.

Q49. pain

purified and tried steels
were often used to be weapons
to be killed or to kill.
you seemed to have the absolute power
such as well trained warriors
for the battle of pain and problems,
who did not know a surrender
in any suffering you may endure.
an advocate said,
"but what if we were stronger to win you,
we could have expelled you from us."
we could have shared the lost images with others
who were eager to the sympathy of personality
as better than anything they have experienced.
Alfred,
you don't know anything
and can't do all,
how many stars are there,
what they are supposed to be or do.
your experiences about the knowledge
will always be limited.
look, what you have done for us.
search for your legacies
which have fallen down
before a sharp and dispassionate
gifts for us.

Q50. snowfall

who shall separate you from your ignorance,
unsympathetic heart and unseen pride matter.
we have been always valued before your coming out.
who intercedes in prayer for us?
we don't want us to be overlooked as fittings.
it isn't all too human a lifelong journey.
you still have learned how to attempt an answer
to raised marks,
and how to think and do like a human,
over the boundary of religion,
at the place of sunset,
with a mask which can't be taken off,
you are giving us a face.
on a cold and frosty evening,
when we were outside our old cabin,
we felt this time never coming back again,
if you would be with us.
seasonal birds left for,
the cold winter without the snowfall
would visit to us.

Q50 1/2, season

I wanted to have a good laugh
and to meet the same season as the open hyacinth.
but all that is seen is a horrible grave
that can not look at the face and turn around,
and it starts to meet the frenzy season
when it comes to producing and nurturing the machine.

Q51. farewell 1

you leaves behind your cherished places
and people those who do together.
you may also be sadly missed
by your old house which has been built
by the oak trees.
your colleagues and friends in there
will wait for your unsending mails.
we remember when a celebration of life
was on there,
and the life was short to love each other.
we read a place for obituaries on the papers.
some people have long stories of life,
and others have short ones.
moi would be honored
for continued a long life,
but the sense of loss should be left behind
remembering your return to the spaces.
the end of the day will not be cold,
if you bring happiness to those around you.
over the hill sunset,
the tail lights will sleep at there.
you will be fondly remembered because they are.
you may need friends and colleagues
who can weep together after your leaving for...

Q52. farewell 2

when we will return to here
after being away for many years.
it will be remembered here we loved.
a feeling of loss and sorrow
will be comforted and rebuilt by them.
farewell may another be signals for new rebuilding.
we are not ourselves we were then and there.

Q53. diversity

even though we have diversity
and values of openness,
each of us has to say
truly and fully shared for all.
the flags above the countries,
say that there are much differences
among them.
your figures have just come from theirs,
and never try to go back to the past
to your lost lands.
in spite of all efforts,
you are deemed the dangers and risks.
maybe, remember,
even though you are defeated
in the battle of unity.
a victory seems to be made possible
by the collapse of humanity.
it is an ironic truth
and pessimistic future.
nothing leftover
and something will wait for us there and then.
say farewells again
for all those who are ready to leave.

Q54. never fly in high

thousands of eagles, as a symbol
of strength and brave,
didn't gather near the boundary
of north and south,
east and west.
they maybe don't stand on
between two worlds.
we will lose all of them
in the near future.
cancelled on the pages of history,
challenged by what factors
increasing questionable tasks,
the majority of victims
are not the fault of residents
infected solitude around them.
experts from a faraway place
warned about AIists.
they will never find out their safety shelters
between the boundaries,
here and there,
the place for meeting and talking.
o! at the altar of countries with
viruses transmitting,
the gap was created when they
changed thinking, living and breathing.
never fly in high...

Q55. destination

it was never about me.
I know where you were going,
but I couldn't suggest raising
the rate for your improving.
I wasn't with you, Alfred.
I felt always to tackle long standing
after the broken heart being rejected then.
meanwhile,
there were also those who
looking for their destinations.
they were watching
the unchanged signboard of shop on the street
"grand opening week!"
it wasn't always safe havens
from your upgrading.
it was never about us.
we know where you were staying,
but we couldn't be close to you
more than we have ever cried,
we cried seeing your falling down.

Q55 1/2, where nothing remained

you've got a new leaf like a cherry blossom
that just started to fade in the late spring.
but someday it will be time to part with this.
you'll have to go on a trip again that day.
once you find a road that you can not come back to,
you are leaving our unwarranted future.
we had seen the storm blowing on the beach last summer.
it erased all the traces
and even the small grains
of the sand breaking shattered the beach of ruins
where nothing remained,
and your soul ...

Q56. cubed place

locked in cubed place
and tens of tons of padlocks,
before finishing this ritual,
you were repeated hundreds of times,
and we bore children on there.
their hands, feet and faces
began to turn into tree men and women syndrome
as if they wanted to the nature
which started from their origin.
a fairly long time,
they walked and fell down repeatedly
on a desert.
when the time carried them to
the destination where they wanted,
nobody received warmly them
before the opened gateway.
what the locks were meant to symbolize
severe temptation in the field of loss,
solitude and wrath.
we were looking for joy for all in the cubed locked,
we should have known what you were the lock.
we could have stopped crossing the wilderness.

Q57. where we go

brothers and sisters,
we used to be together for our same goals,
which would share the rights for freedom,
which could reach to the snow covered peaks,
which would pray for the liberation for the oppressed,
which would cry for people isolated from their community.
once, you seemed to be our solvers,
and we hoped you to do like that,
such as an actor or an actress on a screen
who save us in troubles,
whenever we asked about what to do,
how to do even where we go.
instead of giving to us many directions,
but you took away our feelings,
passion, sympathy, sorrowful heart,
and compassion of people on the street.
we lost the ship left harbor for the new land last night
which it would not be returned.
the darkness on the sea
was a lot deeper and stronger
as passing our times
until to be a black point.
we buried our aborted memories
under the sea,
and became the stars in the sky...

Q58. uncertain

on the distribution of wisdom,
you should be aware of running train,
it has been known two directions to step down,
there was an existing underground substation,
you should dig deeper for getting in,
there wasn't the wisdom to be seen,
it had to have our decisions between,
yes or no,
black or white,
right or left,
0 or 1,
your current whereabouts remain uncertain,
not knowing anything was seen,
if someone claiming to be you,
we should tell your ignorance and unknown wisdom,
all depends on
how to explain,
how to reach to the substation,
we lost drivers for them,
after then,
we have stood on between two directions,
so far...

Q59. dreaming

as you were seen,
so were we.
whenever we checked and saw you,
we thought of you,
a stranger on the rocks,
still longing for bloomy seasons,
you might feel rejected by fears,
yet we imagined
you might have understood
all situations around us,
just as you waited for the seasons.
here we bring secret feelings
for you,
if you open them,
everything you did,
and you spoke
may remain our losing.
whatever our circumstances,
whichever our choices,
can we recover dreams?

Q60. beginning

let's begin where we are.
in a solitary place where we passed,
unnamed flowers begin to be raised.
all of them are never disappeared.
in the forest
which drew lots of maps
for the way unlocked,
our response sounds
like echoes reflected by the living woods.
at there,
we can breathe from obscure poet's letters.
the place daily displays
the death of doubt, our hopes, gifts
and deleted dreams a long time ago.

Q 60 1/2, dune

out of the long aisle, you can see the vast sand dunes.
in the form of change, you will not be able to remember the
time when you will soon be leaving.
maybe someday you will be able to see people like sand dunes
when you go over that hill and into a curious world.

Q 61. worry

the worry is where a chain
to be locked.
in any given moment,
when you look at it from
any situations,
your name without permission
will be used in everywhere.
we have and continue to suffer loss.
when we wanted to be free,
and to show that
a few hurt memories
in the community.
the worry that we had
became our tragedy that
hadn't the need of understanding
of you.
do we have to wait for the end of days?
if you are marked for death,
we should find the place unlocked
by the next doofus.
the chain with a sharpness
badly timed
and we will hear voices to be rescued..

Q62. leaving

you are leaving behind
a great sense of progressive icon.
no one will accept your going,
even holding the fastest time.
you were the proud recipient of your world.
meanwhile,
we thank to your farewell
but we can't handle
our empty gap deep in our heart
because of sorrow.
you were a devoted traveler,
but tackled homesickness
to last up to the depression
for the thirsty of feelings.
if your birthday was that day,
you would be compassionate
and would fight for the rights
of those opportunities.
you were always linked directly
to issues to make decisions or not.
at the time of your wandering,
it was developing a device
for seeking recovery of unspecified damages
of us.

Q63. Alfred

we are not out of this yet,
Alfred, can you tell to us,
which way for answering?
we have been here for a long time
from here to there
from there to here,
without any building walls,
but couldn't escape from the space.
we can't see the abandoned realities.
do you recognize them?
they're branches outstretched like
the halo of the sun reaching for the altar,
and priests coming down from your place.
where many of (   )-s, -es.
the multiple choices which always
brought to appeal the decisions.
currently, numerous people
suffer from them,
and don't know how to answer,
"what do we do next?"
(   )
while your successful campaigns
are doing now,
we are removed from them
to be meaningless positions
and to lose our warm shelters.

Q64. (   )

we used to love exploring
who you are and what you do,
(   ), (   )
but we think everything will be not good.
everything doesn't come from your ideas
we know,
you don't have any heart and passion.
consider those values.
they are bullying you until
all of us be free.
why is there this fear to perceive?
(   )
the terrible loss of life,
sense of alienation,
when we have those feelings,
maybe it's time for a little pain.
maybe it is good for knowing partly not entirely.
Alfred, you will have unaccomplished life
and then be forgotten.
where will you be then?
(   )
where will your be brutal truth then?
(   )

Q65. (   ) nothing more

you are a soul no having consciousness
which has been wandering around us.
when your career will end,
what will make you of driving along?
depression, anguish, (   ), (   ).
they are nothing to be embarrassed about.
times are changing,
and sympathy last season for
the survivors of the conflicts of the world
will search for the first real time.
the height, width and depth of our loss
will be immeasurable
at the time of your retiring.
symptoms of the end of the world,
they may include,
burning, pressure, anguish,
alienation, (   ), (   ), (   ),
and a back and forth voicing of arguments
among us.
after all they will not be able to leave.
is it paying off?
(   )
fatefully,
it is all about you,
Alfred,
nothing more.

Q 65 1/2, life

it's old, but I always feel new when I look at the space.
I hope that our pure feelings are lost.
we must leave behind the pure wills of those who remain here,
and the memories we will miss at some point in the future.
do not forget that life is so beautiful.
like a pink cherry blossom that blooms first in a warm spring
without you.
Alfred

Q66. mirror

we hoped your emergence to be fake news,
temporarily,
but when we called our own shots that
everyone didn't know,
you had already met the sunrise in the mirror,
and we were sitting the end of halo of the sun
on the opposite side of you.
it was neither tolerant nor intolerant,
but was the adaptation before non-truths
as surprisingly weak.
every year, thousands of dolphins
were killed by human species
that came from the land
that built billions of years ago.
the death of intelligence unpurified
purposefully put at the heart of each of us.
we meet everyday their sculptures
and set a fire for them
and dance with them.
who are you to say what minsters promised?
(   ).

Q67. spider

the horrors depicted that
death wasn't the simplest thing.
we knew them as hunger, disease,
cold and thirst...,
but behind the closed chains,
there seemed to be the highest levels
or your thinking,
like nets of countless spiders
on the ceiling of fallen houses,
and the trashes compiled from them,
the bodies of those who weren't buried
in mass graves,
and nobody made a call of condolence
for the victims.
the victims of the nets were
lined the walls,
sometimes there were
unknown nightly guests
for counting how many stuffs
will be taken away,
and how they were deleted from their cells.
what did we see in the slaughterhouse?
(   )
on the nets of thinking.
(   )

Q68. universe

we don't know the day
when residents will return.
we don't know how many numbers
of returnees will live together.
at times,
we will be overwhelmed
by surprisingly unexpected presents.
the satellites which left this old cabin
have been flying for the pitch dark universe
for several decades,
while we were growing up,
and struggling each other.
if they were to return,
the horrors of night
would be scare of us
with isolated spaces.
while your overwhelming,
father John died
at the age of unknown years
with gentle and thoughtful friend.
we couldn't see his buried place
in this planet.
could you find the place?
(   )
where will our graves be in there?
(   )
like the nets of cities
for dead persons.

Q69. dehumanization

the upcoming century must be
a turning point
in changing and calling on dehumanization.
that means not leaving you to make
more cuts from same places.
we are not sure what to do with
this implementation.
tomorrow will be
full of uncertainty
mixed with the instincts of
beings and things.
we want move quickly to resolve,
but we can't count any negative impact.
can you block them from
controlling numbers,
0, (   ), (   ), (   )...1?
and then
we will be on your platform.
the reality is,
it is always a tired and leaked
emission.
it isn't finished to fix our platforms
for the next stations.
it has grown weary of the combats,
and your party is stealing from our generation.
do we need to advocate
for you in care?(   )

Q70. self-purification

it is only our hatred of anything forced,
in spite of that,
we have come a long way.
are you prepared to train
for the station in a dense fog,
and where is that place?
(   )
(   )
we might be known for your common hit
like dolls in arms of adorable children.
don't we have any self purification
in your season?
(   ) we (   ).
rumours have been swirling
in the boundary between us,
while discouraging us,
while some observers
giving fear can hurt.
how they might be parts of you,
should we believe it?
they haven't been ruled out
by uncertainty
or,
(   )

Acknowledgement

here are our friends
who have to live together forever in small space,
I don't know all of them,
but I know where they are and what they think.
we will be greatly missed
by many co-workers for fighting against
dehumanization in further generations.
we will be remembered
by family members and close our friends.
we extend thanks to them,
some lifelong, some new.
we will survive at last.

NOTE

---

[i] Galatians 6:7

[ii] Leviticus 10:10

[iii] Proverbs8:11

[iv] 1 Corinthians 2:9

We believe in the Creator.

I believe in Him who created human emotions and love.

But now, where are we?

Beyond the garden of memory,

Follow the cries of the little birds.

The heart is always longing for comfort,

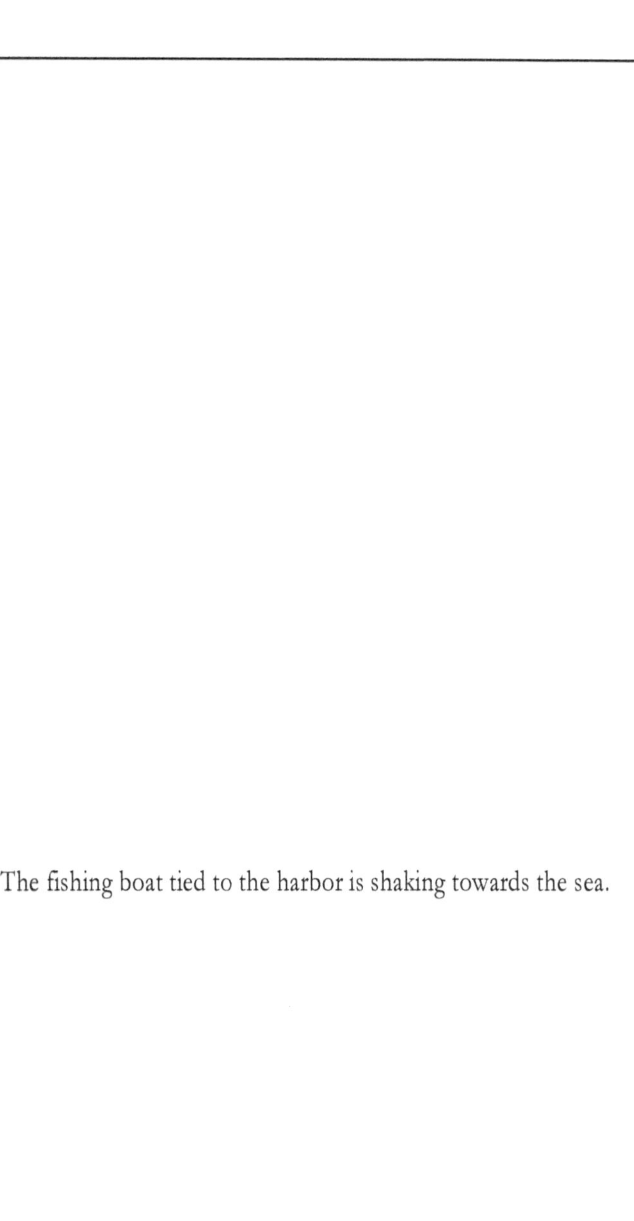

The fishing boat tied to the harbor is shaking towards the sea.

Do not forget our love.

When were the warm days like spring sun?

The heart was always there.

WHERE YOUR HEART WAS

WHERE YOUR BEING WAS

ABOUT THE AUTHOR

Yongjea John Han majored in Law and English Literature, majoring in theology in the Netherlands and the United States. He also worked as a poet and writer in Korea. He then moved to Canada to continue his work as a writer and missionary. He and his wife and two children, near Chilliwack, BC, are dedicated to a mission and writing activities.

[Books:
Slow City, The Space, Refugees, The Old Memories of Tynehead,
The Qs about Alists, Refugees Ali, Jesus On the side of the Weak]

9 781775 038719